T0014563

Look Beyond ...

Ocean of Pain

to Horizon of Purpose

Annie Mac

WESTBOW
PRESS®
A DIVISION OF THOMAS NELSON
& ZONDERVAN

Copyright © 2019 Annie Mac.

All rights reserved. No part of this book may be used or reproduced by any means, graphic, electronic, or mechanical, including photocopying, recording, taping or by any information storage retrieval system without the written permission of the author except in the case of brief quotations embodied in critical articles and reviews.

This book is a work of non-fiction. Unless otherwise noted, the author and the publisher make no explicit guarantees as to the accuracy of the information contained in this book and in some cases, names of people and places have been altered to protect their privacy.

WestBow Press books may be ordered through booksellers or by contacting:

WestBow Press
A Division of Thomas Nelson & Zondervan
1663 Liberty Drive
Bloomington, IN 47403
www.westbowpress.com
1 (866) 928-1240

Because of the dynamic nature of the Internet, any web addresses or links contained in this book may have changed since publication and may no longer be valid. The views expressed in this work are solely those of the author and do not necessarily reflect the views of the publisher, and the publisher hereby disclaims any responsibility for them.

Any people depicted in stock imagery provided by Getty Images are models, and such images are being used for illustrative purposes only. Certain stock imagery © Getty Images.

Unless otherwise indicated, Scripture is taken from the King James Version of the Bible.

Scripture taken from the New King James Version®. Copyright © 1982 by Thomas Nelson. Used by permission. All rights reserved.

Scripture quotations marked (NIV) are taken from the Holy Bible, New International Version®, NIV®. Copyright © 1973, 1978, 1984, 2011 by Biblica, Inc.™ Used by permission of Zondervan. All rights reserved worldwide. www. zondervan.com The "NIV" and "New International Version" are trademarks registered in the United States Patent and Trademark Office by Biblica, Inc.™

ISBN: 978-1-9736-7970-7 (sc)
ISBN: 978-1-9736-7971-4 (hc)
ISBN: 978-1-9736-7969-1 (e)

Library of Congress Control Number: 2019918289

Print information available on the last page.

WestBow Press rev. date: 12/03/2019

The title of this devotional was inspired by King David, who was not pretentious when he penned his journey from pain to purpose. Pain, woe, struggle, suffering, anxiety, fear are experienced by us all, but they do not have to define or design us. We use our pain as a catalyst to draw nearer to God and discover our purposes.

Acknowledgments

First, I want to thank God for granting me the tenacity to do this because writing a book was far more tedious than I anticipated; however, far more rewarding than I envisioned. I would also like to thank my family who were supportive and understanding especially my children Deondre, Logan and Jazmin and my husband Marvin. Thanks for putting up with burnt dinners, writing on napkins and all the other quirks that accompany immersion in writing. I would not be here to share my gift without the time and investment of my grandparents, my aunts, my uncle and my parents, so I am eternally grateful. My sisters and in-laws who said you should do this; you are the best because you never complained when I wanted to share what was swimming around in my head. To my friends in St. Lucia, England, Canada, France, and the US who supported me, I would like to say that your encouragement got me over the hurdles to the finish line. Those of you who read, listened, advised and gave suggestions, I could not have done this without your patience and love. Thanks for sharing your insight and for helping me believe that I was gifted with words worthy of sharing. Additionally, I would like to thank the Westbow team who has guided me through this process to usher this longtime dream into a tangible reality. Lastly, I want to say a grateful thank you to all my readers. When pain and trial visit your corner of the world, in order to discover the purpose, look beyond…

David wrote Psalm 38:1–22 (NKJV) from pain.

O Lord, do not rebuke me in Your wrath,
Nor chasten me in Your hot displeasure!
For Your arrows pierce me deeply,
And Your hand presses me down.
There is no soundness in my flesh
Because of Your anger,
Nor any health in my bones
Because of my sin.
For my iniquities have gone over my head;
Like a heavy burden they are too heavy for me.
My wounds are foul and festering
Because of my foolishness.
I am troubled, I am bowed down greatly;
I go mourning all the day long.
For my loins are full of inflammation,
And there is no soundness in my flesh.
I am feeble and severely broken;
I groan because of the turmoil of my heart.
Lord, all my desire is before You;
And my sighing is not hidden from You.
My heart pants, my strength fails me;
As for the light of my eyes, it also has gone from me.
My loved ones and my friends stand aloof from my plague,
And my relatives stand afar off.
Those also who seek my life lay snares for me;
Those who seek my hurt speak of destruction,
And plan deception all the day long.
But I, like a deaf man, do not hear;
And I am like a mute who does not open his mouth.
Thus I am like a man who does not hear,
And in whose mouth is no response.
For in You, O Lord, I hope;
You will hear, O Lord my God.

For I said, "Hear me, lest they rejoice over me,
Lest, when my foot slips, they exalt themselves against me."
For I am ready to fall,
And my sorrow is continually before me.
For I will declare my iniquity;
I will be in anguish over my sin.
But my enemies are vigorous, and they are strong;
And those who hate me wrongfully have multiplied.
Those also who render evil for good,
They are my adversaries, because I follow what is good.
Do not forsake me, O Lord;
O my God, be not far from me!
Make haste to help me,
O Lord, my salvation!

"Hello, stranger." How profound those two words! I walked into church one Sunday, and that's how a friend greeted me. I went home that day with those words resonating in my head, trying to determine the implication. Yes, I hadn't been in church in a few Sundays. Ironically, I did not receive one phone call to inquire about my whereabouts. Then I had to figure out how many missed Sundays would qualify one as a stranger. Two? Three? I guess it is determined by the one who utters these words for it is relative. "Hello, stranger," suggests an abandonment of sort. However, I was under the impression that a relationship is mutual, mutually beneficial and with each party having mutual responsibility. This led me to my most valuable relationship, the one with Christ.

"Hello, stranger." Does Christ ever address me in that way? I had to think about this and ask God for thought guidance on the matter. This is my conclusion: He doesn't and never will. No matter how long, no matter the depth of my rebellion and disobedience, He knows me by name. He comes to town, finds my street, walks up my driveway to my front door, and knocks. He wants to come in and sup. He doesn't regard me as a stranger; He does not wait for me to make the first move. He, Maker of the universe, not only knows me by name but calls me "child." I am no stranger; I am child. As His child, though, I have the privilege of honoring my Father as the one who gave His life for me. We honor soldiers who fight in wars and defeat the current enemy, knowing that others will arise. However, our Father in Heaven came down, and alone, He defeated the enemy once and for all. How much more should I honor him? He not only did it for me but for all my children, grandchildren, and generations past and present.

I pray that this devotional will increase your fervency in prayer and deepen your relationship with Father, the One who never calls us "stranger." He may be a stranger to me, but to Him, I am child.

Christ is the master artisan
in the areas of refurbishing and recycling,
He takes the wasted life of a man and makes it
the treasured life of a saint.

Day 1
God's Great Design

I may not be a hero who has saved many lives.
I do not own a million, and good food is my demise.
I am not as smart as Einstein; for many things I have no clue.
I am not known by millions, only just a select few.

Mistakes should be my first name, knucklehead my last.
Because of the way I live, my whole life should be a fast.
Decisions, they come quickly before I can comprehend
How I can build a loved one but another easily offend.

Thank God I don't compete 'cause I'd fail almost every test.
I seldom reach the mark, even when I try my best.
But I am oh, so grateful, and I've had to resign
To believe that I am chosen 'cause I'm God's great design.

God's Great Design

> I will praise You, for I am fearfully and wonderfully made; marvelous are Your works, and that my soul knows very well. My frame was not hidden from You, when I was made in secret, and skillfully wrought in the lowest parts of the earth. Your eyes saw my substance, being yet unformed. And in Your book they all were written, the days fashioned for me, when as yet there were none of them. (Ps. 139:14–16 NKJV)

Why don't you always bask in the reality that you are marvelously made?

Do you praise God for making you just the way He did? If you do not, what is preventing you?

Beloved, many of us grapple with the idea that others around us appear to be living their best lives, while we are yet to find our purposes. It is not until we realize that we are all created unlike another, with uniquely designed paths and experiences, that we can begin to fulfill God's plan in our lives. When we spend time envying another's life, we neglect refining the talents with which God has blessed us. This essentially makes us our own dream snatchers.

Remember that when we evaluate the things we like or not, we should form two categories: Things I can change and things I can't.

Things I Can—Do something about them.

Things I Can't—Accept and pray for clarity to decipher why God placed them in your life. Ultimately, God wants what is best for us, so He wouldn't allow anything that would not grow us.

Believe God's Word, beloved. You were wonderfully made! Start seeing yourself as God sees you.

Prayer: With reverence, my Great Creator (1 Peter 4:19), I approach your throne of grace, thanking You for designing me in your likeness. I am blessed to have the Creator of Heaven and earth call me beautiful. I want to start seeing myself, not as the world sees my outward appearance with all its perceived flaws, but as You see my innermost being - my heart. Amen.

> There's no more profound a love
> where a Father willingly accepts the punishment
> for a son He knows is as guilty as sin.

Day 2
Crown for a Crown

An eye for an eye.
A tooth for a tooth.
A hand for a hand.
A foot for a foot.

Convicted and destined to die in a chair
From a trial I never thought was fair.
So horrible the crimes that I'd done,
Didn't want to pay, so I'd been on the run.

I was living my life when I got caught.
My life is now over, was my only thought.
The crimes I committed had hurt even me.
I regretted what I had done was my only plea.

The trial went quickly, no sympathy.
I was a guilty man, 'twas quite plain to see.
Cried out to God to save my soul.
Was willing to yield, to give Him control.

The day I was sentenced was a scary day.
I was sorry for my crimes, but I had to pay.
The judge, He came out; I was going to die.
I had lost all hope and began to cry.

The judge, He did something that caused a shock.
That day, the justice system was rocked.
He said, "You're forgiven; you're free to go.
The crimes that you did no longer show."

Surprised and confused, He must be mistaken.
The judge said it was no error; I had been forgiven.
He said, "Son, while you were committing your crimes,
I had already done the time."

An eye for an eye.
A tooth for a tooth.
A hand for a hand.
A foot for a foot.
A crown for a crown.

Crown for Crown

> Finally, there is laid up for me the crown of righteousness, which the Lord, the righteous Judge, will give to me on that day, and not to me only but also to all who have loved His appearing. (2 Tim. 4:8 NKJV)

Are there times you view God as a condemning judge who waits to pass judgment the moment you fail? Or do you always view Him as a righteous judge and loving Father who has already forgiven the offense? Why?

Talk about the moments you fail at believing that everything in your life will ultimately work together to increase your faith and dependency on God.

Beloved, we have a kind and loving Father who allows nothing in our lives that will be a detriment to us. Start viewing God as the loving, kind, and just Father. We frequently measure God's love with an earthly barometer and miss the mark on unconditional love, which is a difficult concept to grasp. How do we wrap our minds around the idea that Christ died for us to save us from ourselves? God is a judge because sin violates His holiness, but He is a loving and merciful father who gave His perfect life for sinful humankind. Our feelings of insufficiency should lead us to a place of deep gratitude and a commitment to live a life that honors God.

Prayer: Today and everyday hereafter I want to declare that You are my Deliverer (Rom. 11:26), who has shown unmerited favor despite all my selfish and disobedient attributes. You indeed are a God worthy of all my praise. You have taken my crown of sin and shame and replaced it with a crown of righteousness. Thank You for covering all my sins, intentional and unintentional, with Your blood. I am truly perplexed by the enormity of Your love for me. Your unconditional love for me is truly the reason why I fall in love with You over and over again. I love You, dearest Father. Amen.

Don't be so busy chasing tomorrow
that you escape the moments today.

Day 3
Woke Up This Morning

Woke up this morning,
Pleaded for yet another day.
Child, you seldom heed to what your Father says.
You may have good intentions
To always do what's right,
But you reject His Word
And create your own plight.

Read His Word; hear His voice,
Let His spirit guide you.
Read His Word, and let it change your heart.
His voice in the wind tells you He's there always.
Close your eyes, rest awhile,
And talk with Him, dear child.

Woke up this morning.
Thanked the Lord for another day.
Child, do your best to do what His Word says.
Strive vigorously to do what's right.
Heed to His Word for when you do,
You'll definitely see the light.

Read His Word, hear His voice,
Let His spirit guide you.
Read His Word; let it change your heart.
His voice in the wind tells you He's here always.
Close your eyes, rest awhile,
And talk with Him, dear child.

Woke Up This Morning

> Behold, I stand at the door and knock. If anyone hears My voice and opens the door, I will come in to him and dine with him, and he with Me. To him who overcomes I will grant to sit with Me on My throne, as I also overcame and sat down with My Father on His throne. "He who has an ear, let him hear what the Spirit says to the churches." (Rev. 3:20–22 NKJV)

What is hindering you from dedicating your day to God every morning, by seeking Him to guide your footsteps, thoughts, decisions, motives, lips, and passion for that day?

Why is there a marked difference between the days you are deliberate in being led by the Holy Spirit and those where you attempt to go through on your own?

Beloved, listening to the voice of God requires a deliberate slowing of our crazy lives and turning our internal transistors to God's frequency. If you wake up tomorrow, *act* like you have made Him Lord of your life.

A—Acknowledge His presence.

C—Commit your day to Him.

T—Trust that He will only allow what you need.

Prayer: You are my Good Shepherd (John 10:11), who is always there to lead me to springs of living water. Like a stubborn sheep, I walk away from Your guidance, trying to accomplish things in my way and in my strength. I am requesting forgiveness for all the times I have tried to lead the course of my own life without seeking Your wise directives. Lord, help me to be more dependent on You, acknowledging that You are the Shepherd who never abandons or leads His sheep astray. Thank You for being so patient, longsuffering, and forgiving. Amen.

> The prison with the strongest bars can't be seen.

Day 4
Release Me

Melancholy grips my heart
For what once use to be.
Lost innocence as time unfolds
Is an unwelcome decree.

Melancholy grips my life
That time can ne'er repair.
Revelations of wantonness
Leads me to despair.

Melancholy, unleash your shackles
Tied tightly around my throat.
Allow me to breathe awhile,
So I could come afloat.

Melancholy, I am free.
Exposed that you are dross,
Your hold is now reduced; you lie
At the foot of Jesus's cross.

Release Me

Hear my cry, O God; Attend to my prayer. From the end of the earth I will cry to You, When my heart is overwhelmed; Lead me to the rock that is higher than I. For You have been a shelter for me, A strong tower from the enemy. I will abide in Your tabernacle forever; I will trust in the shelter of Your wings. (Ps. 61:1–4 NKJV)

Discuss a time when you experienced despondency or despair, but right at the point where you thought that your "floaties" wouldn't hold you afloat, that Christ revealed Himself in an unexpected and unforgettable way.

Was it a moment that aided in renewed hope, joy, and peace?

Beloved, consider for a minute that during times of melancholy, you allowed a situation, person, or even yourself to become bigger or more relevant than God. Dear one, God is far bigger than any perceivable or unperceivable trial or challenge in your life. He is number one, not only in placement, but in stature and significance. Give God His rightful place in your life. Nourish your relationship with Him rather than feed steroids to your melancholy.

Prayer: On bended knees I come before You, great Purifier (Mal. 3:3). I ask that You purify my thoughts and refine me as gold and silver. One can see the true value of those precious stones only when they are purged of all impurities, so today, I plead to You to cleanse me so that I can reflect Your purity. Help me focus on Your promises so that the joy You have placed in my heart is not snuffed by the cares and worries of this world. Thank You for caring for every aspect of my life. Amen.

> Christ is fully committed to our relationship. The manger—Born in the lowliest of places among the animals. The cross—One of the most painful ways to die among "the animals" are clear demonstrations.

Day 5
Nativity Scene

When you look at the nativity scene,
Do you ponder what it all means?
Do you recognize that it was baby Jesus
Who came to this earth, our sins to redeem?

Do you feel deep gratitude that He left perfect Heaven
To become a menial carpenter's son?
Are you aware that He was ridiculed and rejected
Because He did not have a crown?

Do you understand the magnitude of His sacrifice on the cross,
Where He bled and did die?
Do you know that He is our Savior,
And His gift you shouldn't deny?

Nativity Scene

And behold, an angel of the Lord stood before them, and the glory of the Lord shone around them, and they were greatly afraid. Then the angel said to them, "Do not be afraid, for behold, I bring you good tidings of great joy which will be to all people. For there is born to you this day in the city of David a Savior, who is Christ the Lord. And this will be the sign to you: You will find a Babe wrapped in swaddling cloths, lying in a manger." (Luke 2:9 12 NKJV)

When you think of Christmas, what words come to mind?

How do you approach the Christmas season?

In the spirit of gift giving, Christmas is a time to put differences aside and get together with family. Why is it hard to do that? Share your thoughts.

Do you donate money and time to charities and organizations during the Christmas season? Why?

Is there a noticeable difference between Christmas and the rest of the year with the way you give and serve? Why?

Beloved, the word "Christmas" evokes such fond memories for many people. It is a time when we focus on gift giving and service. The tradition of gift giving was born on the night that Christ was born. Christ, the greatest gift to this world. During this season, carols fill the air, gifts fill stockings, and love for our neighbors fill our hearts. Christmas reminds some of us to live outside ourselves and to bless the less fortunate, hungry, and hurting. If only this contagious sentiment could be extended beyond the Christmas season, then our world as we know it would be a far better place to live. For many, Christmas is a stressful period, where the purchase of the perfect gift has superseded the posture of affection that prompts us to buy a gift for someone. We all need to be reminded of the things that made Christmas truly magical when we were children. The carols; the aroma of cookies, pies, and cakes baking; the family laughter and banter; connecting with friends and extended family; going to church in our best attire; the lights and decorating our Christmas trees; the smell of pine; the stories; the gifts, no matter how small. We need to return to the simplicity, beauty, and magic of Christmas.

Prayer: Thank You for being our Emmanuel (Matt. 1:23), our Father who left His perfect home to come to imperfect earth to die for imperfect human beings. On the night You were born, angels rejoiced. The wise men received the good news that You, Christ, our Savior was born. Earth was about to witness the full measure of love, so complete and profound that we wrestle to fully understand its magnitude. You, our Emmanuel, taught us how we should give to our fellow men and women the love that You demonstrated toward us, but we fail daily. Today, and especially during the season of gift giving, help us to focus on the gifts that money cannot buy. Amen.

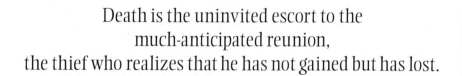

Death is the uninvited escort to the
much-anticipated reunion,
the thief who realizes that he has not gained but has lost.

Day 6
The Coward Death

Death: The word feared by most,
Desired by few,
Given far too much power than deserved.

Death is not the big ogre as esteemed.
In fact, death is a coward, a parasite
Always lurking in the back door of life.

Death is created by life,
Is nonexistent without life.
The sun—life.
The moon—death.

Yet death gets much more attention than life.
It stirs emotions never before displayed.
Once death visits, it causes grief for years.
The void never gone, the pain slowly ceases.

In contrast, glorious life is taken for granted.
Once first experienced, it is joyous; the exhilaration soon fades.
The ecstasy transforms into ingratitude.

Life is no longer celebrated and revered.
It is long forgotten and abused, sometimes even cursed.

Death has been conquered; it quivers in its shoes.
One unselfish act, one undeserving sacrifice by Jesus
Brought the powerful and unconquerable death
Down, down to its knees and shamed.

To be absent from the body, and to be present with the Lord (2 Cor. 5:8).

The Coward Death

> Come now, you who say, "Today or tomorrow we will go to such and such a city, spend a year there, buy and sell, and make a profit"; whereas you do not know what will happen tomorrow. For what is your life? It is even a vapor that appears for a little time and then vanishes away. Instead you ought to say, "If the Lord wills, we shall live and do this or that." But now you boast in your arrogance. All such boasting is evil. Therefore, to him who knows to do good and does not do it, to him it is sin. (James 4:13–17 NKJV)

Who did you lose who was dear to you? Why was it an extremely painful loss?

What was propelling the pain? Was it fear, guilt, regret, awareness of all the projected memories cut short?

Was he/she saved? Did you share the love of Jesus with that person? If yes, talk about it, and if no, what was the reason?

Beloved, death is eminent, and none of us know when it will come knocking on our doors. If you think that death is tragic, let me challenge you to ponder that the greatest tragedy is dying without Jesus. If we truly comprehend that death is a bridge between this life and the eternal glorious life with Christ, then we should be excited about death. Hard concept to grasp? Oh yes. The sorrow should be for those who have not accepted His gift of salvation and those left behind to endure the ills of this life. The day that we were born brought us one day closer to our deaths and eternal life with Christ.

Prayer: Father, I no longer fear death knowing that You are our breath of life (Rev. 11:11). Nothing in this world, including death, is out of Your control. Your power and provisions surpass my ability to comprehend the full extent of Your sovereignty. I know that death is the greatest honor because it is the bridge that transports us from this mortal decaying life to our immortal everlasting life with You. But my heart struggles with accepting death as a blessing because it evokes so much pain and regret, incomplete dreams, and void. Help me, dear Jesus. Strengthen my feeble heart that I can start seeing death the way You see it. Thank you, breath of life. Amen.

As the wind mercilessly deposits leaves,
so do some people who dump truth into our lives.
In contrast, the wind purges,
like others who leave us less cluttered
after making their appearance.

Day 7
Today, My Friend

Today, my friend, you are to me
What water and sun are to a tree.

You are supportive, you give your love.
I know your friendship is rain from above.

And so as you tarry along,
Life can be taxing, but just be strong.

'Cause, friend to friend, I want to be
The kind of friend God gave to me.

Today, My Friend

A friend loves at all times. (Prov. 17:17 NKJV)

Is there a relationship in your life that has withstood the test of time, that "Takes a lickin' but keeps on tickin'"?

Do you recognize the value of this friendship? Have you always?

Address a time in your life when you tried to extend a vaporous relationship beyond its intended time designation in your life. How did things turn out?

In contrast, were you tempted to end a relationship or create distance but eventually realized that relationship was one not meant to be temporary?

Beloved, besides salvation, one of God's greatest blessings to humankind is that of friendship. Deep, intimate, and genuine relationships sustain and encourage us; they strengthen our morales and sometimes may even serve as our lifelines. There are many examples of exemplary relationships in the Bible. David and Jonathan provide a great example of true friendship. We encounter another purely unconditional relationship between Ruth and Naomi. Every relationship is accompanied by differences of opinions and conflict, but as long as those do not demean the value and blessing of the relationship, it will thrive. We are all given the opportunities to develop and nurture lasting genuine relationships. However, we may sometimes be impatient to nurture those relationships and build our many steel walls that are detriments to intimacy. Additionally, there are occasions when we attempt to nurture vaporous relationships. Ask God for the discernment to differentiate between the relationships meant for a period and the ones commissioned to exercise longevity in our lives. If we mix up the two, we may experience heartache or totally miss a blessing. If you do not have at least one close friendship, ask God to help you look in the right place. It may grow from a very unexpected place.

Prayer: Jesus, a friend of sinners (Matt. 11:16–19), You have called me friend and demonstrated the sacrificial quality of friendship. Thank You for caring for every detail in my life. Let me choose to focus every day on the gifts of friendship that have enriched my life whether through positive or negative interaction. Help me to appreciate those whose roots are not deep and get uprooted after the designated season as much as those who are strong and rooted. It is necessary for me to recognize also my responsibilities in friendship, so if I am lacking in that area, I am willing and ready to improve. Thank You, Friend. Amen.

When storms visit our lives,
they not only magnify our vulnerabilities
and inform us that we are truly not
the conductor of our trains,
but provide ample opportunities
for neighbors to connect with neighbors,
families to connect as family,
and man to connect with God.

Day 8
I Surrender

Drowning in a sea of self-reliance,
Determined to be the captain of my own ship,
Never once considered the overwhelming size of the storm.
I was strong, I was prepared, was trained.

Never anticipated that the storm would be
So sudden, so devastating.
And I? Was oh, no match!
I was wrong, I was not prepared, I didn't stand a chance.

I had been captain for so long.
I had worked hard for it, sacrificed for it, earned it.
I had faced prior storms and had survived
A little scathed, a little wiser, a little stronger, or so I thought.

So why am I drowning? Why can't I swim?
I am exhausted for always fighting,
So bitter for not receiving,
So frustrated for not advancing, not reaching
The sandy shore.
I surrender, Lord, I give up.
I no longer want to be captain of my ship.
I may know my ship but can't control the storm or the sea.
But you can, Lord.
Let me lean not on my own limited understanding.
My desire is to totally trust the One who is willing and able.
"Take my life and let it be consecrated Lord to thee."

I Surrender

> Trust in the LORD with all your heart, And lean not on your own understanding; in all your ways acknowledge Him, And He shall direct your paths. (Prov. 3:5–6 NKJV)

Who's the captain of your ship?

Do you recognize God in all your accomplishments? Or do you tend to build your own esteem through your strengths and successes?

Why do you make plans lacking the awareness that you are not in total control and that it's only if God is willing?

Beloved, we read the account of Mary and Martha, and many of us who are doers can identify with Martha's personality. It is not that we should neglect being hospitable hosts who feed our guests for they need to eat. It is the posture of the service that makes all the difference. We should not do anything independent of the awareness of where Jesus is in our lives. We shouldn't put Him on hold to make preparations. We keep Him front and center in all situations. He doesn't require our preparation; He is the bread of life. He doesn't require our preparation; He says, "Come as you are," because He is the One who cleanses our souls. He doesn't require our preparation; He says He is waiting at our door, knocking. Every accomplishment, milestone, triumph, or victory is a blessed gift from God. He designed our brains, gifted us our passions, designed our bodies, and provided circumstances that we can choose to bring Him glory or take all the credit—our choices. The Creator of the universe does not need us to affirm His majesty, but it is foolish to ignore it for we miss tremendous opportunities and blessings. We also miss the opportunities for gratitude in the gifts and humility that accompany the idea that we have received and have not attained in our own strengths. Can we honestly say that we trust our own abilities to plan our lives? How has that worked for you? Place your life in the hands of the One who knows all, sees all, and loves all; the One who can't go wrong and won't go wrong. Surrender is a posture designed to give God His rightful place in our lives. We surrender because we recognize that He is majestic.

Prayer: Dearest captain of the seas, pilot of the clouds, the One who works all things according to the counsel of His own will (Eph. 1:11). It is my desire to surrender to Your will, but sometimes I get in my own way. Help me to understand that surrender does not mean I sit and do nothing. It simply means that I allow You to guide me. Thank You for Your patience as my kinks are sorted out and corrected on life's assembly line. Amen.

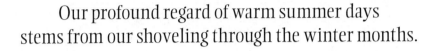

Our profound regard of warm summer days
stems from our shoveling through the winter months.

Day 9
Wonderful Day

What a wonder to behold the glorious dawn
As the sun ushers a brand-new day.
Tranquility makes it possible to be fully engaged with His nature,
His creation,
Before the crazy world awakens to drown the simplicity.
One does not lose hope, though, if this experience was not captured
Since dusk ushers another chance, another possibility to understand
The majestic nature of such a great Creator.
The colorful sunset, the closing of the day, streams across the horizon.
If only all the wondrous miracles were observed throughout the day.

How can one say, "There is no God"?
Beauty left unattended, not cared for, becomes ugly, loses its charm.
How are the colors maintained? Sustained?
How is this beauty constant?
How does it remain if there is no one who keeps it vibrant?
Why does it not fade?

Wonderful Day

In His hand are the deep places of the earth; the heights of the hills are His also. The sea is His, for He made it; And His hands formed the dry land. (Ps. 95:4–5 NKJV)

Why do you roll out of bed dreading the day?

Why do you allow the burdens of the day to outweigh the blessings?

Do you ever stop to simply absorb all the color and beauty around you? Share your experience.

Do you understand that God gifted us with variety so we can get a glimpse of His majesty and power?

Beloved, He demonstrates to us every day that He is no ordinary God. He has mastered every color, design, angle, flavor, and scent. Appreciate the universe around us. Be in awe and wonder of His immeasurable power. We often take for granted the seemingly mundane occurrences in our lives. We do not wake out of bed elated and anxious to see the sunrise. We fail to wait in anticipation of a beautiful sunset, seldom gripped by the chirping of a bird, the flowing waters of a river, the rolling waves of the sea, the perfect droplets of the rain, the unique snowflakes, the crawling caterpillar, the diligence of the ant, the work ethics of the squirrel, the eagle protecting its young, the color on the tulips, the scent of the rose. We often overlook the natural beauty and order of nature around us.

The more aware we become of the handiwork around us, the more we grow to sing praises to our Master Craftsman.

Remember each day to do the vowels

A—Anticipate the gifts.

E—Extend praise for all the variety around us.

I—Identify areas in your life that are lacking gratitude for personal and general blessings.

O—Open your heart and eyes to the wonder of God's creation around you, and remember that people are part of His creation, so enjoy the variety.

U—Understand it is God's desire that we worship the Creator, not the created. When we are in awe of the beauty around us, we should thank God for all His work.

Prayer: Wonderful God, You who formeth the mountains (Amos 4:13), we look at Your creation, and we are in awe of You. Help us never to confuse what was created and who created it, so our praise and worship are lifted to You, our Creator. Thank You for blessing us with nature so diverse, so orderly, so beautiful that it is obvious that there is a designer, a sustainer. God, we worship You for You deserve our praise and worship. We pray that we never take nature's beauty for granted as we seek to grow closer to You. We give You praise. Amen.

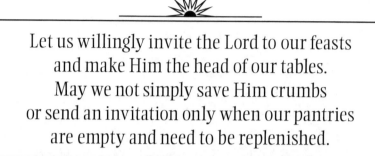

Let us willingly invite the Lord to our feasts
and make Him the head of our tables.
May we not simply save Him crumbs
or send an invitation only when our pantries
are empty and need to be replenished.

Day 10
If

If we claim to have fellowship with Him
Yet walk in darkness, we lie and lack the light of truth.

If we claim to know God,
Yet we are consumed by our own agendas and schedules
Without considering how we can be molded vessels
In His gentle hands, then we are misguided.

If we get more excited to be in the company of celebrities
And feel more honored to be at the Super Bowl game
Than to be on His mission field, proclaiming His grace and promises,
Then we are totally delusional.

If we condemn other religious practices
That worship the created and trust in a "higher power,"
Yet we are so busy pursuing our goals for financial wealth and freedom

That allow no time for us to nourish a more profound relationship
with God,
Then money and success become idols.

If we examine our lives
To assign a percentage of our time dedicated to the things of God,
is it 5 percent, 20 percent, 50 percent, 75 percent?
If God is not in our hearts and on our minds,
On our tongues and in our steps,
In our ways and on our paths,
In our homes and in our workplaces,
In our dreams and in our goals,
In our joys and in our sorrows,
In our today and our tomorrow,
In the way we view ourselves and in the way we view others,
In our youth and in our golden years,
In our blessings and in our trials,
In our sickness and in our health,
In our time of plenty and our time of famine,
Then we have some more surrendering to do.
He requires 100 percent of us, and anything less is not enough.

If

> No one can serve two masters. Either you will hate
> the one and love the other, or you will be devoted to
> the one and despise the other. You cannot serve both
> God and money. (Matt. 6:24 NIV)

Are there areas in your life where Christ does not have full access?

Does His presence extend beyond the confines of the place you gather to worship?

Do you commune daily with Him?

Beloved, I have read Matthew 6:24 on multiple occasions, but recently, something new drew my attention. In this verse, the opposing force to God is not the devil; it is money. I had never thought of money as God's foe, but now that I am a little more mature in my Christian walk, I do understand why. The Bible also states in 1 Timothy 6:10 that "the love of money is the root of all evil." If money is the root, then all evil stems from that money tree, and evil is in direct conflict with the very essence of God's holiness. Now, many scoff at the idea that money can be equated to evil when we can do very little without money, but it is clear that it is the love of it that is dangerous for that love can make us push morality, conviction, and righteous living aside as we begin to compromise, seek loopholes, plot, and plan ways to acquire more. This verse ties into the poem because we have to be controlled by the Holy Spirit and not our desires for materialism and power. God is enough. And if we are blessed beyond the physical, then we have to keep the right perspective and see that His blessing is not simply for acquisition of more to be stored in our own coffers but to use the blessing to fulfill His mission here on earth. Our greatest joys should be centered on the person of Christ, our greatest accomplishments should exist in being involved in the increase of God's kingdom, and our best expense should be the sacrificial giving to ensure that another human being feels the love of God through our generosity. Oh, if only we understand our missions and grasp our purposes.

Beloved, if you are tempted to feel discouraged and inadequate after reading "If," please don't because it is about the ideal. We are well aware that none of us is there yet. However, we need to be reminded that we should not allow other things to supersede the presence of God in our lives. Nor should we be engaged in the mind-set that we can compartmentalize His presence. We can't put Him aside until we need Him, nor should there be areas in our lives where we put up "Private Property" signs for God. He needs full access.

Prayer: Father, thank You for being our Jehovah-Jireh (Gen. 22:14), the One who provides. You are our yesterdays, our todays, and our tomorrows. Our yesterdays teach us that You are enough, and nothing You allow is without reason. Our todays remind us that You have promised to provide our daily bread and all our needs, so we should not worry. Our tomorrows require that we trust that You are going to do what You did yesterday and today. Help us to never take Your love or presence for granted and for us to never get lost in things temporal that allow us to lose our eternal eyesight. We love You, Lord. Amen.

Christianity at its purest, most authentic form
may require that we abandon our religion
to follow Christ.

Day 11
My Soul Yearns

My soul yearns for you, Lord.
My soul cries,
And though the flooding of tears may never satisfy my soul—
It still remains dry like the great Sahara—
My soul yearns for you.

My soul yearns for you, Lord.
My soul bleeds.
Even though this blood I bleed is nothing compared
To your pure shedding of blood on the cross,
My soul yearns.

My soul yearns for you, Lord.
My soul seeks,
and though my soul wanders till it's weary,
it wanders all the way to Calvary.
My soul yearns.

My soul yearns for you, Lord.
My soul finds
Even though my soul is nothing more than the prodigal,

You are still the Father who waits till he returns.
And when He sees him in the distance,
Runs to welcome him back home.
My soul yearns.

My soul cries.
My soul bleeds.
My soul seeks.
My soul finds.
My soul yearns.

My Soul Yearns

> As the deer pants for the water brooks, so pants my
> soul for You, O God. My soul thirsts for God, for the
> living God. (Ps. 42:1–2 NKJV)

Are there times when you just want to slow down and come fully into
the presence of God, just you and Him?

Do you sometimes come to Him in the posture of the prodigal son
or daughter and envision Him being exasperated with you and yet
another mess-up?

Beloved, when I heard the words of this poem in my head, they
came to me as a song. Many of us feel a void in our lives, and
often we cannot articulate what is missing. Sometimes, it feels like a
gnawing restlessness that doesn't go away. Other times, we are aware
that this is due to a break in connection to Abba Father. When we
feel estranged from God, we have to check to be sure we haven't
wandered from His arms of protection, His will for us. We are His

children, and a father never wants his children to break fellowship. He desires consistent worship that is not legalistic or coerced through religiosity. Unhindered and genuine fellowship brings us a greater awareness of our severe condition without God as our first, our foundation, and our center. God does not break fellowship with us, we do. He never turns His back on us as we often believe. He gave His all for us, and even when men here on earth thought that they were executing their plans, we see that their plans ultimately fell into His plan. No plan can ever foil the will of Abba Father. No broken nail, toothache, bad hair day, lost key or wallet, crashed computer, unsaved homework, broken relationship, layoff, unpaid bill, utility shut-off, blown-out tire, snowstorm, hurricane, disloyal friend, hurtful rumor, failing marriage, barren womb, miscarriage, road-rage driver, burned dinner, rebellious teenager, sleepless night, back or neck pain, heartburn, allergy, flooded basement, leaking roof, discrimination, or racial prejudice happens outside God's view. If only we can revisit the lives before us and see how God used unfavorable and painful situations and experiences to work out something for good. If this is not our home, then life here only prepares us for our home. We need to always maintain an eternal perspective to understand God's eternal vantage.

Prayer: Thank You, Jesus, for Your patient love toward us. You are the one who filleth all in all (Eph. 1:23). I am grateful that You are never tired or condemning of me. You are always ready to restore fellowship even when in rebellion I wander to other seemingly green pastures. Thanks for protecting me even then and for Your unending forgiveness and care. Help us to remember that You want what is best for us, and what's best is what's true, and it resides in the light always. So when we feel lost, let us walk toward the light. Amen.

The talents with which we are blessed
are not born from our own inventions.
Rather, they have been inscribed on our lives.
We simply have to discern what they are,
believe that they are,
embrace what they are, and have the gall
to share them with the world.

Day 12
How Dare You!

How dare you not feel blessed!
Did you not open your eyes today?
Did you not see the car out of control because the driver she was sleeping?
You did see, didn't you?

How dare you not feel blessed!
Did you not hear sounds today?
Did you not hear the alarm in your house when the burglar he was creeping?
You did hear, didn't you?

How dare you not feel blessed!
Did your nose not smell today?
Did you not smell the smoke from the grease fire when you were cooking?

You did smell, didn't you?

How dare you not feel blessed!
Did your tongue not taste today?
Did you not taste when the milk you ordered for your child would give the stomach a "lickin'"?
You tasted, didn't you?

How dare you not feel blessed!
Did your arms not feel touch today?
Did you not feel the warm embrace of a loved one even though it was your very last meeting?
You touched, didn't you?

How dare you not feel blessed today!
Did your heart not keep beating?
Did you not keep on breathing?
You are truly, truly blessed because you are living!

How Dare You

> All this is for your benefit, so that the grace that is reaching more and more people may cause thanksgiving to overflow to the glory of God. Therefore we do not lose heart. Though outwardly we are wasting away, yet inwardly we are being renewed day by day. (2 Cor. 4:15–16 NIV)

Are you more apt to engage in complaining or thanksgiving?

Why do you think we complain as much and as often as we do?

Do you think that complaining, whether justified or not, is directly correlated to the depth of our relationship with God? Why?

How can we change our complaining habit to one that focuses more on daily blessings?

Beloved, through my experiences and observations of the world, it is evident that we are more apt to focus on our trials than on everyday blessings. We have developed an entitlement mentality because we expect to wake up every morning, we expect to be well, we expect to drive safely to work, we expect the traffic will be flowing just right, the coworkers will work to their utmost, our bosses will be overjoyed by our diligence, that we will be regarded as valuable assets, and we expect to work eight hours or less. We expect that when we get home, our families will be in perfect sync, and dinner will be enjoyed and appreciated by all. We seldom regard these as blessings, so when a link is broken in our perfect chain of expectations, we become frazzled, irritated, and offended. If we develop the mind-set that waking up is good enough, and everything else is a bonus or blessing, we will be less prone to focus on the supposed offenses. Instead we will focus on daily, seemingly mundane, blessings. To be renewed every day indicates that we have a Father whose goal for us is that we progress daily toward righteousness, so all things that visit our day—whether joyful or painful—will ultimately nudge us in that direction. Daily renewal is an opportunity to grow. But we are often stuck in the same place not because of our situation but, rather, our mentality or thoughts. So my hope for us all is that our minds are renewed every day.

Prayer: Father, You are the One who spoke the world including the mountains (Amos 4:13) into being. Your words are powerful and believable, so help us believe what You speak. You said that we are renewed every day. Help us submit our thoughts to You and not just the areas in our lives that are observable. We need to infuse our minds with truth and to grasp the reality that our behaviors and habits follow our thoughts, so getting our thoughts right before You is key. Thanks for Your Word that lightens our paths, Your promises that strengthen our resolve, and Your love that keeps us in the palm of Your loving hands. Amen.

Satan may win battles but God wins wars.

Day 13
The Word My Armor

Armed with the Word of God,
I am ready for the battle.
I know with all certainty
That the victory is sure.

Armed with the Word of God,
I am ready to face temptation.
You have promised in Your Word
That You've given the "way out" door.

Armed with the Word of God,
I am ready for the devil.
Though he aims his darts of sin,
Jesus offers the cure.

Armed with the Word of God,
I am ready to face the world.
And when I am hurting from lack of love,
I love my Savior more.

Armed with the Word of God,
I am ready to face myself.
For though I am a tough contender,
With His Word I can mature.

Armed with the Word of God,
Hallelujah, I can resist.
The devil will flee; I have the promise.
It's been done many times before.

The Word My Armor

> The night is nearly over; the day is almost here. So
> let us put aside the deeds of darkness and put on the
> armor of light. (Rom. 13:12 NIV)

Do you daily clothe yourself in the armor of God?

Do you realize that protection extends to your head, heart, hands,
feet, eyes, ears, and tongue?

Are you aware that you are in battle, and that, though the ultimate
battle has been won on your behalf, there are many wars that you
will need to fight?

Do you understand that your unpreparedness does not only impact
your life but those around you? Do you feel a sense of responsibility
to those around you? If you don't, why not?

Beloved, it is often said that the best offense is a good defense. This can
be applied to our spiritual lives, and as we all know that temptation is
a never-ending phenomenon, we must be on guard at all times. For a
Christian, the Word of God is the best weapon because it is the armor

that's able to help us withstand the endless darts that are hurled at us daily. Imagine a real soldier who goes into enemy territory and decides that, despite the cannons and bullets he sees being hurled and the fact that he sees his fellow soldiers are wounded because the enemy is well equipped with ammunition, he decides to disarm and not take cover. It would be suicidal and irresponsible, not simply because he is putting himself at risk, but he also fails to protect his comrades. Many will view it as unpatriotic, and this person will be viewed as a traitor. If we have to apply the same principle to our spiritual life/battles, which are the most important wars we are going to fight, we have to view it with the same convictions. We need to get suited and armed every day with the Word of God for if we don't, we are spiritually suicidal. We also have a responsibility to our fellow soldiers by "covering them" in moments when they are weakened or their safety is compromised. This is done by speaking biblical truth and promise into their lives, and this can only be done if we daily gird ourselves with God's armor. We often look to soldiers as our heroes for they demonstrate incredible bravery and self-sacrifice. We honor their sacrifice and remember them individually and collectively. But dare I say that we need to extend the same sentiment to those who have fought many spiritual battles on our behalf. Let us take a moment to recognize and pay respect to our many unsung heroes.

Prayer: Father, thank You for your assurance of victory if we gird ourselves with Your Word. Thanks for being our shield (Gen. 15:1). There are times when we feel weak and overwhelmed by the tasks set before us, but we want to remember that we are not alone. You have provided the weapon and a plan of defense. But sometimes in our desire to bring ourselves glory, we are compromised behind enemy lines. Forgive us for all the times we neglect to do what we know is wise, chasing our own paths that often lead to no exits. Help us to trust Your design because we know that there is no one better, to believe your Word—the lamp that guides our paths and the light that shines the way. Amen.

One Creator—limitless designs, no lemons.

Day 14
I Fit

Though I may be vertically challenged and packed one suitcase instead of six for the journey,

I fit!

Though my brushes and combs are no match for the mop on my head,

I fit!

Though my natural winter coat does not shed in the spring,

I fit!

Though everything on my body heads south during all four seasons, and not just for the winter as do birds,

I fit!

Though the sizes in my wardrobe and the Australian kangaroo can share notes on their leaping abilities,

I fit (even though they don't)!

I fit! I fit! I fit!

I fit in God's universe, in his plans!

$\mathcal{I}\,\mathcal{F}it$

> "For I know the plans I have for you," declares the
> Lord, "plans to prosper you and not to harm you,
> plans to give you hope and a future." (Jer. 29:11 NIV)

What makes you often feel inadequate, and when do you wish that
you could change your circumstances?

Why do you sometimes struggle to fit in your own skin, whether it's
from weight, race, physical feature, and so on?

Beloved, what a beautiful promise from the Lord. The Bible teaches
that we were formed in our mothers' wombs (Jer. 1:5) by the hands
of our Savior. He who formed us has a plan for us. God says that He
knows. Not that He guesses or "hopes" like we do. He knows the
plans; they are set in stone. His plans are always there to increase us.
We sometimes equate God's idea of prosperity with materialism or
monetary gain. However, Jesus said that it is easier for a camel to go
through the eye of the needle than for a rich man to go to Heaven
(Matt. 19:24; Mark 10:25; Luke 18:25). This indicates that prosperity
would not be a stumbling block for us because it is God's will that
"none should perish but all come to repentance" (2 Peter 3:9). So as
far as monetary prosperity, it is not one that all can handle. Often,
it is the catalyst of one's demise. True prosperity is the ability to take
the blessings from God and honor Him with the resources with which
we are blessed. It is about being good stewards, generous, humble,

and kind. Yes, we were formed in our mothers' wombs with purpose, unique abilities and talents, and unique placement in family and community. There are some of us who wonder why we didn't get to pick our parents. Why this family? Really, God? Well, as unbelievable as it seems, God also orchestrated that to bring Him glory. However, that can only be achieved if we can envision His will in all things. Yes, God makes no mistakes! We have a wonderful future that is not limited to life here on earth but an eternal fellowship with our heavenly Father. Let us learn to use our deficiencies, shortcomings, and life challenges to demonstrate that in our weaknesses, He is strong. We do not have to be defined by our deficiencies. Rather, let us be characterized by our Christlikeness though never perfect.

Prayer: Father, we are gripped by the beauty and blessing of a baby being formed in a mother's womb. You have said in Your Word that it is You who formed us in the womb (Isa. 44:24). Thank You for creating each one of us with a unique purpose. Help us remember that You formed us with specific assignments and experiences. May we never lose hope or sight of Your will, which is to ultimately bless us in ways that will bring us closer to You. Help us to embrace who we are because You created us as we are. Thank You for uniquely placing me where I was born and to whom I was born. Help me never forget that You create nothing without any purpose. Amen.

Our truest lives are in dreams awake.

Day 15
Created to Be Free

Lord, let me step out of my box.
Help me tear down my walls.
Remove all the mountains that I didn't have to climb.
Eliminate the pain that I've made come my way.
Break the shackles; they were never meant for me.
Help me understand my soul was created to be free.

I've taken my calm lake and made it into a tumultuous ocean.
With the rain of Your blessings, I've caused a raging storm.
My beautiful gardened transformed into a deep, dark jungle.
Shimmering snow into an avalanche transform.

Lord, help me to step out of my box.
Help me tear down my walls.
Remove all the mountains I didn't have to climb.
Eliminate the pain I've made come my way.
I want to trust You despite what I think I see.
Help me understand my soul was created to be free.

Created to Be Free

> I will walk about in freedom, for I have sought out
> your precepts. (Psalm 119:45 NIV)

Do you approach life from an optimistic or pessimistic perspective?
Do you see the problems and fail to regard them as opportunities?

Do you feel freedom in Christ? Why?

Beloved, many of us walk around laden with guilt though we have
laid our lives at the feet of Jesus. We feel the sting of sin that we have
asked God to forgive and often take back the sin after it has been
forgiven. Where is the joy of the Lord? It is stifling under the veil of
shame. Our strength is joy, and if we approach life from the point of
view of self-condemnation, we become weak and ineffective. Now,
does that mean that we are reckless and lackadaisical in the pursuit
of a righteous life? Absolutely not. But we need not fall into the trap
of self-condemnation either. So the next time you are apt to beat
yourself up for a sin already forgiven, let us remember that His mercy
is plenteous (Ps. 86:5). God created a breathtaking universe for us to
enjoy and to illicit praise and worship that ultimately leads us to a
place of joy. Let us every day surrender our lives so our joy may be
full. Let us tap into our strengths and experience the joy of the Lord.

Prayer: Heavenly Father, You are our blessed hope (Titus 2:13).
Lord Jesus, convict us daily to make You Lord of our lives so we can
enjoy fountains of joy, rivers of peace, and oceans of love. God, help
us understand that You created us to be free, not to have the right to
do all that we desire but the privilege to be free from the bondage of
sin. Thank You for revealing Yourself to us and for gifting us Your
Holy Spirit that lives in us and sets us free. Amen.

Go; Slow; No—God's MO

Day 16
God's Traffic Light

You must be quite familiar
With the good old traffic light.
But when you're in a hurry,
You wish it would take flight.

You gratefully welcome its presence.
You know it's for your own good.
But when you're running late,
"Traffic light, I'm not in the mood."

Sometimes when you want your way,
From the route you deviate.
"I don't think so, you traffic light.
You're not going to make me late."

The traffic light placed on your route
Is exactly what you need.
You may be rushing to your death.
There's sometimes detriment in speed.

And so when God's green light says go
After being on your knees,
You proceed confidently and unabashed,
Knowing it's God who you please.

But when He sends the yellow slow,
You accelerate your speed
Instead of slowing to understand
How He wants to lead.

So next time you encounter
The green, the yellow, the red,
Think not that it is an inconvenience
But, rather, the cause of its design instead.

God's Traffic Light

> LORD, I know that people's lives are not their own; it
> is not for them to direct their steps. (Jer. 10:23 NIV)

Friends, do you ever feel like there are days where nothing is going right?

Did you ever make plans and they fell apart before you even realized they were dismantling? Share.

Beloved, I am not sure how you feel about plans that fall apart, especially after you devoted some time to making sure that all ducks were aligned in a row. However, if you are a type A personality like me, you probably have one of these incidents every week. Another area that serves as a huge stressor is when we took measures to be on time, but it felt like the universe conspired against us and everything that could go wrong, did go wrong. Of course, it is a great attribute to be timely, but when we have adequately prepared and, for odd reasons, things fall apart, we have to conclude that there must be a reason. I am not condoning the behavior of the habitual tardiness to which we fall prey for that is indicative of bad time management. Rather, I am addressing the times when we plan to be early for a job interview, a child's play, a game, a wedding, funeral, concert, exam, flight, and so on, where being on time is key, but we did not anticipate the unseen things that delayed us. This is extremely hard to do, but if in those moments we simply remember that God is in control, we trust His omniscience, and recognize that there is reason in all things, we should maintain our composure. Perhaps that day there was a bigger lesson than punctuality; maybe it was self-control or patience. Additionally, we do not know the many instances we are delayed because God is protecting us from an unforeseen undesirable circumstance. So the next time plans fall apart, let us remember that we serve a God of fine details. He designed the details for the butterflies, so He is concerned about the details of our lives. Trust Him.

Prayer: Our Father, you are our El Roi (Gen. 16:13), the great God who sees all. It has been sung that if Your eyes are on a sparrow, we know You are watching us. Thank You, God, for caring about every detail in our lives. Help us to remember that when things are seemingly falling apart, they are falling in place, even though it makes no sense to our human reasoning. We pray for hearts that trust Your will, what You allow, Your provision, and providence. Thank You, Father. Amen.

Life is way too short.
Don't wait for one set of eyes to close before yours open.
Don't wait for another's heartbeat to be evicted
before yours get convicted.

Day 17
Goodbye, Ginny

The loss of a friend so profound, so deep,
I felt the despair over my body creep.
I was hot, I was cold, felt like I was going to be sick.
And all of a sudden, my life seemed quite bleak.

I remember the day that I heard the news.
Couldn't process what I heard; I was so confused.
Why was she chosen? It was such a loss.
She's never coming back, to humanity such a cost.

I know I was at a crossroads and had to choose well.
The crying, the hurt would be intense I could tell.
Knowing that she was gone would surely be a test.
But I knew she would say, "You must try your best."

And now as I reflect on the life that she once lived,
She was an exceptional mother, wife, and friend I believe.
I chose to keep living and do extra in her name.
Even though it hurts less, I love her the same.

Goodbye Ginny

> To everything there is a season, A time for every purpose under heaven: A time to be born, And a time to die; A time to plant, And a time to pluck what is planted; A time to kill, And a time to heal; A time to break down, And a time to build up; A time to weep, And a time to laugh; A time to mourn, And a time to dance; A time to cast away stones, And a time to gather stones; A time to embrace, And a time to refrain from embracing; A time to gain, And a time to lose; A time to keep, And a time to throw away; A time to tear, And a time to sew; A time to keep silence, And a time to speak; A time to love, And a time to hate; A time of war, And a time of peace. (Eccl. 3:1–8 NKJV)

Have you ever lost someone close? If so, was it sudden, or did you have time to say goodbye or prepare?

Did that death really test your faith, or did you immediately conclude that although you did not fully understand why, you were going to trust God to help you through the pain?

Did you feel anger toward another during that process? If so, who and why?

Beloved, losing someone to death is painful. The Bible teaches that there is a season for everything, including death, but none of us look forward to the season of losing a loved one. We have such phrases as, "gone too soon," "another one bites the dust," "pay the ultimate price," and a host of others, but all bare the void and scars that death inflicts. I lost my friend Ginny suddenly several years ago. That really jogged my reality because she was healthy and awesome and died suddenly one night in her sleep. To this day, I still have sleep issues, and it is only as I pen this devotional that I realize it is because of her passing. Death impacts us in unforeseen ways, and I didn't anticipate how I would be affected. Confounding the pain was the fact that I had not returned a telephone call from Ginny, believing that I would eventually. Well, that opportunity never came, and for that, I am forever regretful. One cannot talk about death without talking about what we should not do while we still have breath in our bodies. We should not neglect to tell our loved ones how we feel, we should not neglect to work things out when there is conflict, we should not fret over minute things, and we should not take life or others for granted. Additionally, we should honor our loved ones by the lives we choose to live once they are gone. In Psalm 116:15 it says, "precious in the sight of the Lord is the death of his saints." God looks at death as something pure, not as painful, as we see it. Sometimes when one is sick, we pray for healing and never anticipate that some healing is in the form of death. Death is only painful if we are estranged from our Creator because, "to be absent from the body is to be present with the Lord" (2 Cor. 5:8).

Prayer: Father, You are called the Author of Life (Acts 3:15). You write our stories, and we are blessed to have the opportunity to live them here on earth. We understand that You give us life and that this is not our permanent home. So when You call our loved ones home before us, we pray that we seek comfort in Your arms of grace and healing even though we do not understand why. Help us to appreciate each day as a gift and to live a life that brings honor to You and our loved ones who now bask in Your presence and glory. Amen.

Purpose wilts without the rain of passion.

Day 18
Let It Burn

Time, you know, will reveal God's desire
For He has blessed me with what the journey requires.
I look beyond the horizon blue,
And in my heart, I feel that this is true.
I was created to be great, you'll see,
'Cause no one can foil God's plan for me.

There's a fire in my tummy.
Let it burn, let it burn.
Sprinting forth to lands unknown,
Let it burn, let it burn.
And if you try to get in God's way,
His will He's apt to relay.
There's a fire deep in my heart.
Let it burn.

I do believe that God wants the best for us.
I encourage you to not put up a fuss
When your life is driven by the I,
And you forget why He came to die.
God knows your every trial, every pain.
Without them, by His side you won't remain.

There's a light in the darkness.
Let it shine, let it shine.
Touching hearts in lives unknown,
Let it shine, let it shine.
And if you like to have your own way,
Surrender that control to God today.
There's a light in the Word,
And it's the Son.

Let It Burn

Never be lacking in zeal, but keep your spiritual fervor, serving the Lord. Be joyful in hope, patient in affliction, faithful in prayer. Share with the Lord's people who are in need. Practice hospitality. Bless those who persecute you; bless and do not curse. Rejoice with those who rejoice; morn with those who mourn. Live with harmony with one another. Do not be proud, but be willing to associate with people of low position. Do not be conceited. Do not repay anyone evil for evil. Be careful to do what is right in the eyes of everyone. If it is possible, as far as it depends on you, live at peace with everyone. Do not take revenge, my dear friends, but leave room for God's wrath, for it is written; "It is mine to avenge, I will repay," says the Lord. On the contrary: "If your enemy is hungry, feed him; if he is thirsty, give him something to drink. In doing this, you will heap burning coals on his head." Do not be overcome by evil, but overcome evil with good. (Rom. 12:11–21 NIV)

Why do you allow circumstances to impede your zeal for the Lord?

Have you allowed those who have hurt you to change you? Why or why not?

The Bible teaches that we are to be kind, loving, and generous to our enemies. Is that an easy admonition? Why?

Beloved, I am normally a high-spirited individual. However, there are days when I allow circumstances to obstruct my view of God. It is atypical for us to continue to extend generosity, kindness, and consideration to those who hurt us, especially if it was deliberate or from negligent or disregard. The more I read the corresponding verses for today, I am convicted on how hard my heart has become toward those who have hurt me or others. It is easy for me to be kind to those who are hurting, those who mourn, and those who are hungry. But if those needs fall upon the shoulders of people who I perceive as "evil," I feel less sympathetic and see it more as a consequence that is being rightfully administered. The quandary is that there are no preconditions where this principle has to be administered. We are to be like Christ. Though many propose that it is easy, it certainly isn't. Unless you have experienced profound hurt from something like molestation, murder of loved ones, assault, physical/mental abuse, bullying, defamation of character, and so on, you cannot propose the effortless posture of living like Christ. It is a daily acknowledgment of the need to surrender our wills, feelings, and inclinations to Him. The love and fervor to which we are called are no small feat, but it is the standard set before us that reminds us of our inadequacies. However, there is hope that our lives are in a constant state of growth and maturity till the day we die if we allow Christ to work in us.

Prayer: Oh, faithful Father, You have called us all to a place of continuous joy. You have defined our strength as your joy (Neh. 8:10). May we, Father, be mindful that though life's circumstances challenge our sense of peace, we should always return to Your promises and build our lives on Your Word. Lord, there are people who have hurt us profoundly, and the idea of being kind to them makes us want to puke. But You commissioned us to exercise kindness and generosity toward them. So we ask that You help us give what our hearts want to hold; help us feel where we have grown cold and care where we are struggling to extend love as You would. Thank You, Father. Amen.

God is the best gift giver.
The best—salvation,
the next—freedom of choice.

Day 19
God's Empty Vessel

You've often heard the saying, "Empty vessels make the most noise." When I was growing up, it was taught to both girls and boys.

But dare I say that what we sometimes learn is based on another's perception.
And as we study God's Holy Book, He gives us a more profound education.

You see, in God's Word He clearly states that He needs us to be empty.
It is when His spirit fills our empty hearts we can finally have the victory.

He wants us to His vessels be, so in His hands, He shapes and mold us.
It may sometimes cause us pain but are encouraged to yield and not fuss.

This adage and meaning depends largely on how you choose to view it.
The Bible recommends we empty ourselves; before to God we submit.

So next time someone says something ill about empty vessels and noise,
I hope you will articulate that empty vessels are the most wise.

God's Empty Vessels

> In your relationships with one another, have the same mindset as Christ Jesus: Who, being in very nature God, did not consider equality with God something to be used to his own advantage; rather, he made himself nothing by taking the very nature of a servant, being made in human likeness. And being found in appearance as a man, he humbled himself by becoming obedient to death—even death on a cross! Therefore God exalted him to the highest place and gave him the name that is above every name, that at the name of Jesus every knee should bow, in heaven and on earth and under the earth, and every tongue acknowledge that Jesus Christ is Lord, to the glory of God the Father. (Phil. 2:5–11 NIV)

Have you ever felt like you were empty from feeling inadequate?

How do you attempt to be refilled?

Do you realize that the only lasting filling is the one offered by God's Holy Spirit?

Beloved, if you are feeling inadequate or like something is lacking in your life, you are in the best place. For it is in our inadequacies that Christ can show up and do the filling; it is in our time of want that He can become the One who makes us complete and full. Often, we search for temporal fillers, but how can we fill eternal beings with temporal things? These filler bandages, temporary in nature, do not provide real or lasting solutions. We have to go to the real source of sustenance to be filled with living water. Christ said that those who drink from His living water will never thirst anymore (John 4:14). If we believe that we are our own providers and little islands unto ourselves, there is no room for God to do His work in us. Beloved, the best place any of us can be is in the hands of our omnipotent Father, who is Alpha and Omega, the beginning and the end. Allow Him to do the filling for He is the only One who tailors full-proof fillers. Please consider one more thing. Being filled is not always a pleasant process. For example, if you are someone who needs to be filled with the fruit of patience, God is going to do the filling by providing situations where patience is produced. In like manner, if you are someone who lacks kindness, God will send circumstances where kindness will be developed. Are the situations always pleasant? No, for they are going to make us uncomfortable and test our resolve and go against our grain. However, they are necessary for filling for when we are full, we are complete and live with purpose.

Prayer: Elohim, You are the One who created the universe and hung the stars, and placed the sun and moon in the sky (Gen. 14:18–20). They follow Your will and design. Help me remember that You designed me in the same manner to operate optimally, according to Your will. Father, I recognize that when I attempt to live my life in a fashion where I think I know what's best for me, You consistently remind me that I am Your child. Thank You for caring about the wayward child. God, I come before You empty, so You can fill me with Your living water and Your fruit—love, joy, peace, patience, kindness, goodness, faithfulness, gentleness, self-control. I understand the filling is not always easy or pleasant but necessary for me to bring glory and honor to Your holy name. Thank You, Father. Amen.

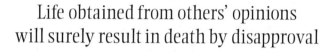

Life obtained from others' opinions
will surely result in death by disapproval

Day 20
How Many Times?

How many times have you denied Him?
How many times have you dishonored His name?
The cock has crowed three times,
But in sin and shame you remain.

How many times have you denied Him?
How many times have you dishonored His name?
You witnessed when He restored the blind man's sight,
Yet you depend on other things to ease your pain.

How many times have you denied Him?
How many times have you dishonored His name?
You won't believe until you see His nail-pierced hands.
You choose to be a passenger on a runaway train.

How many times have you denied Him?
How many times have you dishonored His name?
You continue to judge Adam and Eve for their disobedience,
But you continue to cover your sins in shame.

How many times have you denied Him?
How many times have you dishonored His name?
You fail to realize that once you become His son or daughter,
Even when you mess up, He loves you just the same.

How Many Times?

> They profess to know God, but in works they deny
> Him, being abominable, disobedient, and disqualified
> for every good work. (Titus 1:16 NKJV)

Have your actions stated denial or dishonor to the Father, who wants what's best for you?

Do you agree that perfect love does not give up on us or deny us, and that imperfection, fear, and rebellion in our hearts are what foster the practice of denial?

Beloved, we have all denied Christ in one way or another. However, it is easy for us to see the denial in another, but when it appears in our attitudes, actions, and motives, we are more prone to qualify them as otherwise. None of us are perfect, and consequently, we often say no to Christ. We need to engage in self-reflection daily, so we can confess the areas or moments that we have denied full access or control to God. Often, these are not the blatantly sinful areas but those gray areas or seemingly non-Christ areas like the conversations in which we engage, the things we laugh at, the movies we watch, the places we go, the wasteful time we dedicate to social media, the music to which we listen, and the friends we keep. It also includes serving in ministries simply to pump our pride, hate and prejudice that we harbor in our hearts for specific people and ethnic groups and the disdain we feel toward those in different political parties other than our own. Beloved, we are asked to be vigilant because we battle powers in high places (Eph. 6:12). We misjudge the method of battle and are often unprepared for Satan's craftiness. Let us not deny Christ in areas where we now recognize the methods by which this denial occurs.

Prayer: El Shaddai, God Almighty (Gen. 17:1), we are a broken people who continually reject Your perfect plan in pursuit of our own imperfect plans. And though these plans often explode or implode, we continue to operate under the guise that our lives are somehow in our hands. Oh Jesus, we are a rebellious people who try to manipulate and control our own destinies but are reminded over and over again that ultimately, we can do nothing that will foil Your plan. Let us move to the rhythm of Your will, to build where You instruct and tear down where You direct. Help us to make Your words the sails of our yachts, catching the wind in the direction of Your will. Amen.

> My love for another
> has to mean more than tears at a grave.
> It must be experienced when he or she is able
> to see it, eat it, hear it, smell it, feel it.

Day 21
Wake Up, My People

My people, wake up!
Wake up from your slumber.
Wake up because the harvest is full.
The night draws to an end.
The day dawns to new opportunity,
Yet your hibernating sleep swells, like the waves during high tide.

My people, wake up!
It is time to lead the blind.
They wander through the maze of corridors with cemented exits.
There is no light, no water, no food to feed their eternal souls,
So the eminent slow decay leaves carcasses strewn across the hallways.
The unbearable stench drenched with the sweet aroma of lilies
Cannot mask this abominable reality.

My people, wake up!
Aren't these your neighbors? Your friends? Your sisters? Your brothers?
Do you really understand, My people,

That if your people die before becoming His people that they will
never become our people?
It is too late once the curtain has been dropped.
There is no intermission, no second call.
The season ends, and a new baby play is onstage.

So, My people, do not tarry.
Do not be sluggards.
There is much work to be done with every precious minute.
Love like you were commanded, My people.
Modeled for you, My people.
It will give your faith new legs,
Legs that are strong, faithful, and sure
That will shatter Hussein Bolt's record in a hundred million pieces.
The urgency is real; the stakes are high.
Will you continue to sleep? Relax? Chill?
Or will you get up and go do your good Father's will?

Wake Up, My People

> To the angel of the church in Sardis write: These
> are the words of him who holds the seven spirit of
> God and the seven stars. I know your deeds; you
> have a reputation of being alive, but you are dead.
> Wake up! Strengthen what remains and is about to
> die, for I have found your deeds unfinished in the
> sight of my God. Remember, therefore, what you have
> received and heard; hold it fast, and repent. But if
> you do not wake up, I will come like a thief, and you
> will not know at what time I will come to you. (Rev.
> 3:1–3 NIV)

Who is a missionary?

Do you understand that when you accept Christ's gift of salvation, you automatically become a missionary?

Make a note of all the family and friends who have not accepted Christ as Lord and Savior. These are the people who make up your mission field.

Do you realize that you are placed in a specific position of influence for the kingdom of God?

Beloved, many of us walk around asleep though we are awake. God's desire for our lives is that we are awake, on fire for the cause of the kingdom. We have become indifferent, lackadaisical, and self-absorbed. We are to think of ourselves as being in the army of God. As brothers and sisters, we do not simply leave our comrades in battle and save ourselves. We fight alongside them, we shield them, we don't give up until all are accounted for; sometimes this accounting requires our lives. Yet we are nonchalant where our brothers' and sisters' souls are concerned. We simply step over bodies that are wounded, though we have the power to contribute to saving them. We have become desensitized at the horror of lost souls, so the world continues to operate in chaos and sin. Brothers and sisters, God did not call us to individually change the world, but He expects us to be warrior neighbors, siblings, coworkers, children, and so on because we are at war.

Prayer: Heavenly Father, thank You for winning the war on our behalf. You have said that the battle is Yours (2 Chron. 20:15). Help us to recognize that we still need to perform in spiritual battles, not just for ourselves, but on behalf of family, friends, neighbors, and strangers. Help us snap out of our passivity because that, too, is not

Christlike behavior. Lord, we want to sacrifice like soldiers, to fight like warriors, and to love like brothers. One day we look forward to the proclamation of "Well done, thou good and faithful servant," but help us recognize there was action that preceded those encouraging words. We pray for hearts that love, hands that feed, feet that will go the extra mile to proclaim that You are our one true God, who died for all people so no one had to die. Thank You, Jesus. Amen.

You are what you eat.
You are what you speak.
You are what you do.
Yes, those all reflect you.

Day 22
Example

Have you considered the word "example" and what it embodies?

This word "example" stands on a solid rock, and though the storms of life toss it to and fro,

it stands.

It is born from a tiny mustard seed and slowly grows into one of the most majestic trees that provide nourishment, a home, and a place to rest from the scorching sun.

Example has lived a life on earth and has challenged men and women, boys and girls to live their best lives yet, to do what's right, no matter how others may view them.

Example is not afraid to shine its light, to feed the poor, to wipe the tears of the suffering; it rejoices when a man gives his heart to the Lord no matter how horrible the wrongs he committed in the past.

Example, sweet Example, you are worthy to be praised; you teach us to love those who are unloving, uphold the truth, walk along paths that are seldom trodden, impact the world, to be strong and courageous.

We are called to be examples—to be set apart, a city on a hill, a path to His cross, no diluting, no more blending, no more compromising, called to be children of God. Called to be

Examples.

Example

> Let no one despise you for your youth, but set the believers an example in speech, in conduct, in love, in faith, in purity. (1 Tim. 4:12 NKJV)

Who has been an example for you?

Do you consider yourself a good example to those around you? Why or Why not?

If you considered that you were created by God to be an example to those around you, would it change you in any way? What would you do differently?

Do you agree that Christ is our greatest example? Why or why not?

Beloved, when we think of examples, we often pick heroes we admire. However, we have to be careful that admiration is not wasted on qualities or accomplishments that do not emulate the person of Christ. When we look to qualities that are admirable, let us start in a manger and journey to the cross. Both are entrenched in the muck of humiliation and stench but contain the greatest demonstrations of love that our human minds can fully process. Examples are not people who climbed a ladder while trampling on others but those who stayed grounded to make sure that those climbing did not topple over. Examples are not simply those who have had opportunities to have a dream discovered and recognized but those whose dreams, though buried in their hearts, are still able to take their realities and make that their dreams. Examples are those who understand their purposes because God placed at least one on our lives. And if God placed it, don't you think it is to reflect His will and mission in some way? Let us not get lost in the glitz of examples. Let us be inspired by the simplicity of *the* Example.

Prayer: Gracious Father, perfect example (John 13:15), why do we falter and chase after flawed examples when You came to show us the perfect way, perfect truth, and perfect life? God, we want to be examples, not as the world defines, but to be men and women who clothe ourselves in love, joy, peace, patience, kindness, goodness, faithfulness, gentleness, and self-control. For it is in this fruit that our souls are nourished and we grow. Help us remember that our fruit does not only nourish us but also is intended to be a delight to and have an impact on the ones with whom we come in contact. God, we want to be like the man who was a king but walked as a pauper, who built mansions but had no home, who drank but was the well, who ate but was the bread, who died but life was in Him. Thank You for being that man, that God, that Example. Amen.

Don't trade your identity
for another's indemnity

Day 23
No Mistakes

Lord, I'm tired of running, tired of the daily race.
Life is hard, full of trials, disappointment.
Friends and family can't seem to fill the space.
Feel lost in my own skin, resent the life I inherited.
Don't want to be rich, but less is not enough.

I am enough.
Don't search any longer.
I am enough.
Repeated words make meaning stronger.
I am enough.
False beliefs make you a self-wronger.
I am enough.

Went to church and heard the preacher say
We are the perfect fit, rough around the edges, though.
All of us in need of some grinding before the shine.
Sometimes painful, but in me, You've begun a good work.

I'm where I need to be, see what I need to see,
Feel what I need to feel, touch who I need to touch,
Laugh how I need to laugh, cry how I need to cry,

Live how I need to live, love how I need to love.
And at the end, on the mountaintop, discover the reason for the climb.
God, You make no mistakes, absolutely no mistakes.

No Mistakes

> For my thoughts are not your thoughts, neither are your ways my ways, declares the Lord. For as the heavens are higher than the earth, so are my ways higher than your ways and my thoughts than your thoughts. (Isa. 55:8–9)

Do you ever feel like you are living someone else's life?

Have you ever felt like your life circumstances or the people in your life were mistakes?

Have you ever questioned God's purpose in your life? Why?

Beloved God does not make mistakes. If He did, He wouldn't be God. However, we do mess up on occasion. Let me challenge you to consider that even your mistakes are not a surprise to God and since, "all things work together for good to them that love God, to them who are called according to his purpose" (Rom. 8:28), nothing, absolutely nothing happens without purpose. So now you are thinking of some things that have happened to you and question their purposes in your life, things that you wish you could erase from the whiteboards of your life. Perhaps you have been cheated, maligned, abused emotionally or physically, lost a job, underwent a period of financial anorexia (or are in the midst of it right now), suffered physically, or lost a loved one. Yes, these things are horrible and some things unimaginable, but if we can sometimes see beyond the pain or challenge, we see the silver lining to hope and blessing. Bad things happen to good people all the time. If it didn't, then we would be more prone to the art of attempting to manipulate God with our goodness and more prone to judge others if something bad were to visit their lives. Approximately two thousand years ago, a perfect man was beaten, bruised, and shamed for crimes He didn't commit. He died a shameful death between thieves as His mom's heart broke at the foot of His cross. Yes, bad things happen to good people, and though we do not always have the privilege of revelation, God is always present. So stay strong, and instead of asking why, ask how, and know that with God, all things are possible.

Prayer: All Sufficient Father (2 Cor. 9:8), help me to always remember that You are generous and kind, especially when life circumstances attempt to derail my faith. Help me, Father, understand that to every physical action there is an equal or greater spiritual reaction. Help me to trust Your sufficiency and to never think of myself or anyone else as a mistake. Help me value each person, each experience as You see them—no mistake. Lord, we acknowledge that You allow everything with a purpose. Thank You, Father. Amen.

The measure of a man
is contingent on the stature of his praise
despite the depth of his thorn.

Day 24
Endure and Enjoy

How would we experience joy if at first did not endure the pain?
What would give rise to that emotion if we did not understand the gain?

It is through the constant struggle that our hearts cry out in misery.
We seek out a place of refuge, where we could to it flee.

Then when the quake of sorrow sets in and our hearts respond in gloom,
We accept the fate before us and decide to erect the tomb.

Then suddenly, a rainbow hovers over, and things begin to turn around.
Faint hearts secures a faster rhythm at the prospect that the missing link will be found.

Then sweet joy comes into existent; it can no longer be shackled down.
It understands the endless torment and so in our honor, decides to wear a crown.

So when you're in that place of sorrow and life's outlook is extravagantly bitter,
Endure as best you can the trial; it only makes joy so much sweeter.

Endure and Enjoy

> Weeping may endure for a night, but **joy cometh in the morning**. (Ps. 30:5)

Have you ever prayed for relief from pain or woe that did not come immediately? Share.

Have you had to persevere through a situation or event and thought that you could not bear the pain for another second, but you did?

What did that do to your faith?

Beloved, a life with Christ is not devoid of pain. But the most amazing promise is that all pain is only for a season; it won't last forever. God, in His matchless grace, never allows us to endure more than we can bear, so there is no need to fret. "God is good all the time," has become a catchphrase, but it goes without saying. Our overabundant use of this phrase makes me wonder if it is an attempt to convince ourselves, or do we think God needs our validation of His goodness? He is good, no matter the condition of the hearts of humans, the circumstances, the downs, the tests, the failures. The right view of God will aid in the right view of our circumstances.

Prayer: Father of rainbows, lights at the ends of tunnels, silver linings, and joy in the morning, we attempt to honor You as equally as You honor us. Father, You gave us night and day, a perfect demonstration that life is cyclical and nothing lasts forever, not even our pain. Father, You said that You are God who comforteth those who are cast down (2 Cor. 7:6). God, You are our promise, our morning star, and we love You. Amen.

Behind every cloud are the blue sky and radiant sun.
In time, the wind will blow it away.

Day 25
Witness

Perplexed by the enormity of the trials raining down over my head like an April's rain.

The paths landscaped with goldenrod, not my desire, not my morning cup of tea.

Most days, the sun chooses not to rise. The dark, stifling and thick, robs the clarity—the vision.

The torturous loneliness engulfs my entire being, and I find myself dangling over the valley of despair.

Then, out, way out in the darkness, I see a tiny light.

Small but nevertheless a light.

The light seems suddenly to multiply.

There are hundreds, thousands, countless, dancing in a rhythm that I cannot comprehend.

But I am mesmerized, captivated, focused.

All the tiny lights begin to converge, and as they do, the light grows stronger, brighter, more powerful.

Till all I see is one great light shining, almost blinding,

Dispelling the darkness that was heavy and thick.

And I—I know that forever, I am changed.

I feel it deep within, and I am at peace.

Witness

> "Believe in the light while you have the light, so that you may become children of light." When he had finished speaking, Jesus left and hid himself from them. Even after Jesus had performed so many signs in their presence, they still would not believe in him. (John 12:36–37 NIV)

Have you ever entered an unfamiliar dark place and discovered that simply flicking the switch was an arduous task because you could not find it?

Did you eventually realize that the switch you were looking for is voice activated, and all you had to say was, "Jesus"?

Do you realize that we carry God's light in us when we choose to make Him Lord of our lives?

Beloved, one of the biggest assaults on humanity is loneliness through isolation. God designed us to be in relationship with others. It is what sustains us. It is no coincidence that depression and suicide are on the rise because, though we are under the impression that through social media we are more connected, we are, in fact, more socially disconnected. Relationship requires more than simply having fingers engaged. It requires intonation, touch, eye contact, facial expressions, body language, and individual quirkiness. God designed vertical relationships for it's where we draw from His great light. Once we receive His light in us, when we become His children, we have the privilege to radiate His light in us. This we do through our horizontal relationships here on earth—a vital element to our physical survival. The more mature our vertical relationships, the more radiant our horizontal relationships. So if we are struggling with our horizontal relationships, we need to take vertical stock.

Prayer: Yahweh Yireh, our God who provides, thank You for being our light, a "lamp unto our feet and a light unto our path" (Psalm 119:105). God, who would we be without You? Where would we be without You? Thank You for saving us from the darkness and for speaking light into our lives. You took Your perfect light and made it accessible to us through the perfect love of Your Son. Thank You for Your provision and paving the way for us to have access to You. Amen.

> The power of the plot lies in the mystery.
> The power of faith lies in the certainty of mystery.

Day 26
Radiant Sun

The radiant sun shines and warms the earth,

Ushering the day's grandeur.

And while it's here, it makes its presence known.

The clouds come in, but the sun can hold its own.

No clouds in the sky can terminate its light.

Oh, what a great wonder, the secret of its might.

And when at dusk we wave our sad goodbyes,

The moon reveals that its presence is lasting in the sky.

Radiant Sun

Then Jesus spoke to them again, saying, "I am the light of the world. He who follows Me shall not walk in darkness, but have the light of life." (John 8:12 NKJV)

Have you ever pondered on the fact that God is ever-present, never asleep, never tired, never frazzled?

Share some moments in your life where the presence of God was more apparent than others.

Do you realize that even if God's presence is not blazing in your life, His light is still shining, and He still reminds us that He is there?

Beloved, sometimes a relationship with God requires, on our part, that His presence be a blazing light, but we need to understand that He is God of amazing and God of subtlety. When God does a miraculous and grand thing, I worship Him in honor. But when God shows up in the minute details, I am in awe that He dedicates time to the seemingly insignificant things. Different occurrences may cause us to question His presence because they are difficult to process, but He is that light that never fades and the Father who never gets it wrong. I am learning that we often do not see God's light because of the dimming by our intellect. It grieves me that people have been hurt by "religious" people and somehow implicate God in their flaws as if He made them do it. I am also saddened by the fact that many equate God to religion, when Christ made it clear that it is solely based on a relationship with Him. It has often been said that "Religion is man's way to God, but relationship is God's way to us." Oh, if we could set aside our intellect and recognize that even the brain was designed by God. His light shines on this earth whether we choose to acknowledge it or not, and He is the source of all honorable and holy things. My hope for you is that you will see His light as it illuminates upon this earth. I also pray that you feel His light as it moves you into a closer, deeper, richer relationship with Him.

Prayer: Father, thank You for being our light and salvation (Ps. 27:1). Father, with so many ideologies and worldviews today, help us sift through our opinions and make our way to truth. Oh, God, much of what we believe is solely based on human opinions, and we, in blind faith, believe. However, it is so hard for some to believe Your perfect Word to us. Oh, God, do a great work in our hearts and help us to receive Your light and for Your rays to radiate into our families, neighborhoods, and communities. God, please help us as we continue to follow Your light. Thank You for being our eternal Father. Amen.

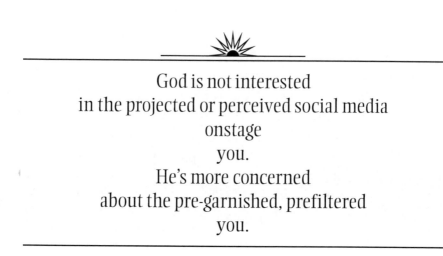

God is not interested
in the projected or perceived social media
onstage
you.
He's more concerned
about the pre-garnished, prefiltered
you.

Day 27
Your Love Is All I Need

Forsaking all others, I run to You.
No longer do I want another
My heart belongs to no one else
Your love is all I need.

Sorry that I wasted so much time.
Sorry that I did not clearly see
Your love is forever.
Your love is all I need.

I run to Your everlasting well,
The one that fills me up.
I am never thirsty; my cup overflows
With Your love, oh, God.

I am never letting go.
Your amazing love is true.
No longer do I want another.
My love belongs to no one else.
Your love is all I need.

Sorry that I wasted so much time.
Sorry I did not clearly see.
Your love is forever.
Your love is all I need.

Your Love Is All I Need

> You shall not make for yourself an image in the form of anything in heaven above or on the earth beneath or in the waters below. You shall not bow down to them or worship them; for I, the LORD your God, am a jealous God, punishing the children for the sin of the parents to the third and fourth generation of those who hate me, but showing love to a thousand generations of those who love me and keep my commandments. (Ex. 20:4–5 NIV)

Have you ever wondered why the Bible uses the word "jealous" in the context of God? Do you see the pairing as an oxymoron, knowing that we are serving a perfect God?

Do you lack the understanding to decipher between God's jealousy and ours because jealousy is a sin?

Do you think that God's jealousy is motivated by circumstances different from ours?

Beloved, God is the sinless Father. When the Bible refers to God as "jealous," it is addressing the practice of idol worship. God created us primarily to be in communion with and to worship Him, so when we sinfully worship another person, place, thing, or experience, we are in violation of God's purpose. God's jealously cannot be equated to those ill feelings that we on occasion experience. Worship belongs to God and should be solely given to Him. Let us consider a husband and wife relationship. A husband and wife are out on a date, and another man looks at his wife and thinks that she is stunning. The man openly flirts with the wife, who is obviously enjoying the attention. The husband gets angry because jealously kicks in. Is his jealousy justifiable? Absolutely. He is the only one who has the right to flirt with his wife. The husband's jealousy is also not sinful because he is the only one who has a right to flirt with his wife. In like manner, God's jealousy is right because He is the only one who should receive our worship. The Bible teaches that anything or anyone that takes the place of God in the area of worship is an idol.

Prayer: Father, You have said that You are a jealous God (Deut. 4:23–24). Lord, it is clear in our words that we cannot serve two masters. You and You alone should be Lord. You have admonished us to put You first in our lives, but we often put people, things, places, or ideas in Your place. God, I am sorry and want to put You in Your rightful place. Thank You, Father, for being long-suffering toward me. Help me to every day make a conscious decision to surrender my will to You, to put You first, to make You central. Thank You, Father.

If we learn it wrong, we will live it wrong.
And if we live it wrong, others will learn it wrong.

Day 28
Not Enough

A young child growing up saw a lot of ugliness around.
Ignition of a desire to make a difference was born.
I grew up and dedicated my life to humanity;
A humanitarian is what I aspired to be.
So like Mother Teresa, who put all her needs behind,
I would travel the world, and the impoverished I would find.

I did it not for recognition or conceit.
I did it and would not accept defeat.
Determined that my life would a blessing be,
I would make a difference, leave a legacy.

I travelled the world and saw lots of pain,
Challenged governments who had abandoned the poor to increase their gain.
Rallied the rich, the churches, general public to get involved,
To pledge to remain vigilant until world hunger was solved.
Would not settle until all women had gained equal rights.
No was not an option; for justice, I would endure the fight.

Then one day I was confronted, kneeling before the Lord.
He clearly whispered, "My sacrifice you will never be able to afford.
You have made a difference in this life to fade away.
But what about eternal life, which we must all face someday?"

Not Enough

> Then Jesus came to them and said, "All authority in
> heaven and on earth has been given to me. Therefore
> go and make disciples of all nations, baptizing them in
> the name of the Father and of the Son and of the Holy
> Spirit, and teaching them to obey everything I have
> commanded you. And surely I am with you always, to
> the very end of the age." (Matt. 28:18–20 NIV)

Are you a humanitarian at heart? On what projects have you
embarked?

Were the projects successful? In what way?

Do you connect your acts of service to the love of Christ?

Do you realize that the best gift to others—above food and clothing,
freedom and safety—is salvation?

Beloved, instrumental service requires that one extends a vision
beyond this temporal existence to eternal life. The best kinds of gifts
are the ones that lead a child of God to the Father, and successful

humanitarianism is the one that addresses present needs within the context of his/her eternal reality. Having empathetic eyes to see the woes of another and commit to engaging one's passion, time, and resources are depicted in the example of Christ. The Bible says that our lives are like a vapor, here for a short while, so we cannot focus more on the short life here and neglect to prepare for the eternal one that we are promised. That would be irresponsible and costly. So let us have a heavenly earthly view.

Prayer: Heavenly Father, You are the One whose name should be proclaimed over all the earth (Ex. 9:16). Lord, there are times when I allow the approval of others to feed the place where You alone should reside because I take the credit for Your blessings and the areas that You plowed. God, please help me to remain humble and, when I am given the opportunity to sow seeds, that I do not get tempted to accept praise when those seeds sprout. Today, God, my desire is that Your will be carved on my heart, stamped on my hands, and guide my feet. Let me never lose sight of my purpose. I want Your command to become my daily conviction. Let my love for the lost be greater than my own agenda. Help me hold fast to Your Word that reminds us that Your desire is that none should perish. Father, I know that many who are heading toward eternal separation from You are not interested in seeking Your will or are sure that their way is what works. Help me to be kind and patient. And when my testimony is challenged and ridiculed, help me to continue to equally love. Amen.

We give so much thought to the
enemies that surround us
that we neglect to slay those within us.

Day 29
Certainty

Armed with the Word of God,
I am ready for the battle.
I know with all certainty
That the victory is sure.

Armed with the Word of God,
I am ready to face temptation.
You have promised in Your Word
That You've given the "way out" door.

Armed with the Word of God,
I am ready for the devil.
Though he aims his darts of sin,
Jesus offers me a cure.

Armed with the Word of God,
I am ready to face the world.
And when I find myself unsure,
I love my Savior more.
Armed with the Word of God,

I am ready to face myself.
And though I am a tough contender,
With His Word I can mature.

Armed with the Word of God,
Hallelujah, I can resist.
The devil will flee from me.
It's been done many times before.

Certainty

> I have kept my feet from every evil path so that I might
> obey your word. I have not departed from your laws,
> for you yourself have taught me. How sweet are your
> words to my taste, sweeter than honey to my mouth!
> I gain understanding from your precepts; therefore I
> hate every wrong path. Your word is a lamp for my
> feet, a light on my path. (Ps.119:101–105 NIV)

Do you realize that the Word of God is a gift to you? How do you
treasure that Word?

Do you comprehend that God left a blueprint for successful living?
How successful do you feel? Why?

How intimately do you know God?

Beloved, although there are many battles that we face on a daily
basis, I have often said that our biggest opponents are ourselves.
God knew that our flesh would be one of our greatest struggles, so

His Word admonishes us to keep our tongues "bridled," to guard our hearts and minds, and to pay special attention to lust, pride, envy, judging others, slothfulness, and so on. God in His wisdom also knows that left on our own, it would be very difficult for us to overcome temptation. So He always provides a way out, if only we would deduce His escape route. The problem is often we change God's exit door from temptation to a revolving door. We escape and often reenter the same door to revisit the same temptation that may cause us to sin. The benefit of having Christ as Father is His incredible quality of being patient. He never gives up on us. When our relationship with God is severed, it is not on account of His abandonment. Rather, it is due to our choice to withdraw from His arms of grace. God is the patient Father, who seeks and rescues us, but He will not do so against our will. We have to take the initiative to enter into His rest, and once we do, we have the responsibility to guard our hearts and minds with His Word.

Prayer: Father, you are the One who delivers us from evil and provides all we need to survive our day (Matt. 6:11–13). When we feel unsure of ourselves, help us to rely on Your perfect understanding, Your omnipotence and omnipresence, Your majesty and power, and Your hope and peace. Thank You for providing Your Word, which assures us that you are always our shield, our way out, and our reason. There isn't any battle, Father, that is beyond Your insight, Your power, or grace so when I am in the valley or on the mountaintop, You are able. You are the One who rights all our wrongs, who erases the numerous scuffs on our brilliant white walls that you painted. Thank You, Jesus.

Sometimes God will take you to the banks of the Red Sea
with the enemy's mighty army encroaching.
And there He will demonstrate that He will not take
you to it without having a plan to get you through it.

Day 30
Significance

He is weaving something beautiful in my life.
He is weaving something glorious in my heart.
A basket to hold beautiful treasure,
A blanket to keep someone warm,
He is weaving something beautiful in my life.

Beautiful things woven begin with a thread
That follows a path unforeseen.
It meanders and moves by the hands who create
Until the beautiful pattern is revealed.

The thread, it must learn how to stand out in a crowd,
Or sometimes disappear or stand still
To allow another to take center stage.
It's the only way the beautiful picture is filled.

So when you see a thread, don't you think
That he is less significant than he is.
You just never truly know how his beauty will glow
Until the masterpiece is no longer concealed.

Significance

I thank my God every time I remember you. In all my prayers for all of you, I always pray with joy because of your partnership in the gospel from the first day until now, being confident of this, that he who began a good work in you will carry it on to completion until the day of Christ Jesus. It is right for me to feel this way about all of you, since I have you in my heart and, whether I am in chains or defending and confirming the gospel, all of you share in God's grace with me. God can testify how I long for all of you with the affection of Christ Jesus. And this is my prayer: that your love may abound more and more in knowledge and depth of insight, so that you may be able to discern what is best and may be pure and blameless for the day of Christ, filled with the fruit of righteousness that comes through Jesus Christ—to the glory and praise of God. (Phil. 1:3–11 NIV)

Have you ever felt insignificant?

Do you battle with self-worth?

Is there anyone in your life who corrodes your value? In what way?

Beloved, our Father does not create faulty merchandise. Along His assembly line called life are many opportunities for Him to refine the beautiful people He made in His image. I think of the endless debate on nature versus nurture and examine life from God's vantage as best I can with my eyes of mortality. God created us in our mothers' wombs, so from a nature's point of view, we are created perfectly. However, this does not mean without physical challenges because we are part of a fallen world. God in His majesty nurtures us through circumstances in our lives; these may be physical, relational, circumstantial, and financial. You may wonder how perfectly created beings need to be perfected through circumstances. The fact is, in addition to being nurtured by the bountiful hands of our Father, we are also nurtured by parents, institutions, family members, peers, neighbors, television, social media, music, books, and so on, which do not always correlate to what God's Word says. Dare I say that nurture here on earth sometimes draws us further away from God and His declaration of who we are. There are many entities that purport that we need fixing, but this is often solely based on physical attributes or circumstances. This is based on what we can see and evaluate. In contrast, God is concerned about our spiritual well-being. He works on our hearts without necessarily changing our circumstances. God comes into our lives and restores us unto Himself. He takes the pieces of our scattered puzzle pieces and forms a beautiful masterpiece.

Prayer: Gracious Father, You said that we are created in Christ Jesus for good works, which God prepared beforehand so that we would walk in them (Eph. 2:10). Even before I was a fetus, You were shaping my body, my gifts, and my purpose. You, oh God, created me and placed me in the family of Your choice. You chose my features and even took the time to number the hairs on my head. Father of the rising and setting sun, the One who put the stars in the sky, thanks for making me in Your image. Help me remember when I doubt my worth that You see me as a masterpiece. Thank You for perfecting and preparing me to be in the home where I can dwell eternally. Thank You, Jesus.

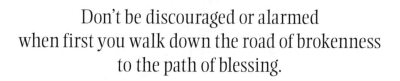

Don't be discouraged or alarmed
when first you walk down the road of brokenness
to the path of blessing.

Day 31
Not Taking No

Waking up every day, sun's up, earth's full.
Feel like today's the day; ain't gonna be a fool.
But the cloud of despair and defeat settles in quite fast,
And the feeling of strength and drive quickly fades, quickly passes.

I am not taking no for an answer.
Not accepting no when the Lord has said yes.
I am not taking no for an answer.
Not saying no when the Lord wants to bless.

It's been so long; world says that I have not been strong.
Didn't know how to respond, to tell them they're just wrong.
It was easier to buy into the lie,
But at night, I'd break down and cry.
Need to find a way to break the chains.
In this place I can't remain.

It's been so long since I believed.
It's been too long my blessings I received.
No longer standing in God's way,
Simply claiming what He has to say.

No longer cursing other's life films.
No longer chasing other's dreams.
Not seeking permission for what the Lord has endorsed.
Not waiting another day; it's been a tragic loss.

I am not taking no for an answer.
Not expecting no when the Lord has said yes.
I am not giving no for an answer.
Not saying no when the Lord wants to bless.

Not Taking No

> For no matter how many promises God has made,
> they are "Yes" in Christ. And so through him the
> "Amen" is spoken by us to the glory of God. Now it is
> God who makes both us and you stand firm in Christ.
> He anointed us, set his seal of ownership on us, and
> put his Spirit in our hearts as a deposit, guaranteeing
> what is to come. (2 Cor. 1:20–22 NIV)

Are you ever unable to move or make a decision because you are
afraid that you will make a poor one? Why?

Do you understand that there is a correlation between obedience
and blessing?

Many equate blessing to materialism, but can you think of and list
other ways that we are daily blessed?

Do you trust God enough to know that your life is in His hands and that He is capable of providing all you need?

Beloved, I pray that in Your life, the voice of others may not trump the leading of the Holy Spirit. It is egregious if we allow others to place us in their constricting boxes of expectation. Do not allow others to rob you of the life that God endorsed, the experiences that He would like you to enjoy, or the places He would like you to go. Seek God; He will guide you. He has left many promises in the Bible for our edification, for comfort, and to attain peace and joy. In His Word, He also teaches us how to address fear and self-esteem issues that may rob us of the blessings He has awaiting us. God is a generous Father who gives His children good gifts. He challenges our views of Him by asking if we, imperfect beings, give our kids good gifts, how much more a perfect Father. Laced in uncertainty, we often park in our thoughts and miss the blessing of walking out in faith. Beloved if only we exist in the freedom and certainty, "that all things work together for good to those who love God." What an amazing life we would enjoy. Far too often Christians believe that a life with Christ is one that is spent in penance or one that has eradicated fun and laughter. God's desire is that we enjoy His amazing universe that He created. His design is breathtaking if we practice observation. He certainly created it to be enjoyed and experienced. Engage your senses—all of them. In this era of technological advances, the average person overuses the sense of sight to interact with the world, but the other senses are not utilized as much. Let me challenge you to daily use the sense of touch (touching a phone or remote doesn't count), taste something different, go outside and awaken your sense of smell to the touches of perfection that God placed around us, and listen to the sounds of nature. Beloved, no longer should you take no for an answer to where God leads. Step out in faith. Enjoy this gift of the universe with which we were so generously blessed.

Prayer: God, You are our good Father, the One who says yes according to Your will (John 13:13–14). Help me, Lord, to trust Your voice more than I trust my weakness or fear. I would like to claim Your promises and walk out in faith, knowing that You have paved the way for me. Develop my trust in You when I allow the opinions or approval of others to overpower Your leading, Your chastening, Your Word. Part of having, "your word as a lamp unto our feet and a light unto our path," is relinquishing our limited views of the world to the One who is Alpha and Omega (Rev. 21:6–7). Today and tomorrow, I would like to commit my insecurities, my fears, my slothfulness, my procrastination, and all the things and habits that rob me of the fulfilling life that You promised. I am encouraged by Your faithfulness toward Your children. You never give up on me. Thank You, Father. Amen.

Beloved, God loves you no matter what you believe or how you feel. His love and mercy are not contingent on how you respond to Him or view Him. He loves you all the same, and the Bible teaches that if we call on His name, He leaves the ninety-nine behind that are in His fold to chase after the one. Yes, His love is immeasurable; yes, His love is enough; yes, His love covers all our sins, and yes, no matter how badly you think you messed up or how deep your pain, God already has considered how He is going to carry you through it. The horizon is captivating for it is there that the sun sets, bringing in a time of rest that elicits healing. And when we are healed from rest, the sun rises to extend new perspective, opportunity, and a chance to start over again. The horizon, beloved, is a reminder that nothing is constant. If you ever become despondent and worry begins to set in, all you have to do is look to the horizon.

Do not await the occasion to be told
you are able,
you are loved,
you are unique,
you are special,
you are treasure,
you are beautiful,
you are complete,
you are capable,
you are worthy,
you are jewel,
you are safe,
and experience despondency
because affirmation is a
stranger or an infrequent guest.
You have already been told
by the Creator,
and His opinion of you
should outweigh all other.

David wrote Psalm 138 (NKJV) on discovering His purpose.

I will praise You with my whole heart;
Before the gods I will sing praises to You.
I will worship toward Your holy temple,
And praise Your name
For Your lovingkindness and Your truth;
For You have magnified Your word above all Your name.
In the day when I cried out, You answered me,
And made me bold with strength in my soul.
All the kings of the earth shall praise You, O LORD,
When they hear the words of Your mouth.
Yes, they shall sing of the ways of the LORD,
For great is the glory of the LORD.
Though the LORD is on high,
Yet He regards the lowly;
But the proud He knows from afar.
Though I walk in the midst of trouble, You will revive me;
You will stretch out Your hand
Against the wrath of my enemies,
And Your right hand will save me.
The LORD will perfect that which concerns me;
Your mercy, O LORD, endures forever;
Do not forsake the works of Your hands.

Printed in the United States
By Bookmasters